NLP

Discover Your Maximum Capability Through Simple Neuro-linguistic Programming Strategies

(Utilizing Neuro-linguistic Programming For Social Influence)

Alistair Daniels

TABLE OF CONTENT

The Framework Of Neuro Linguistic Programming 1

Mind Governance: Who Provides Guidance In Shaping Your Thoughts? 11

The Fundamental Tenets Of Neuro-Linguistic Programming 23

The Mental Computer 46

Integration Of Parts 53

NLP And Self Talk 72

What Capabilities Does Neurolinguistic Programming Possess And What Are Its Limitations? 76

Foundations Of Neuro-Linguistic Programming 82

Embarking On The Path Of Weight Loss 92

Strategic Method For Enhancing Self-Assurance 103

The Efficacy Of Communication Lies In The Reaction It Elicits. 110

How To Substitute Negative Experiences With Positive Counterparts 115

The Insights 122

NLP Methodology: Effective Message Delivery
.... 125

Utilizing The Technique Of Self-Hypnosis For
Efficient Internal Communication 132

How To Deal With Fear 143

NLP Within Business 150

The Framework Of Neuro Linguistic Programming

Within the contents of this chapter, you will acquire knowledge in the following areas:

Present strategic approach
Procedure or Operation
Anticipate Future Developments
- Terminate the Neuro Linguistic Programming Frame
- Inaugural Neuro Linguistic Programming Frame
- Neuro Linguistic Programming State
- Neuro Linguistic Programming Condition
- Neuro Linguistic Programming Stage
- Neuro Linguistic Programming Mode
- Neuro Linguistic Programming State of Mind

Neuro Linguistic Programming Result
- Establishing Rapport through Neuro Linguistic Programming

Introduction

Neuro Linguistic Programming (NLP) pertains to the domain of personal growth and advancement. Nevertheless, in distinction to any other methodology within the realm of personal growth, Neuro-Linguistic Programming (NLP) employs practical frameworks derived from the experiences of exceptional individuals across various domains of the human condition. Therefore, Neuro Linguistic Programming is not amorphous and lacks practical application.

Furthermore, Neuro Linguistic Programming employs the faculties of the senses to enhance and enhance one's perception of the objective world. Furthermore, it has been evidenced that NLP serves as a proficient means to unearth the latent abilities of an individual. Therefore, the methodologies and tactics employed in this field will facilitate the practitioner in achieving their objectives with comparatively greater ease.

Ultimately, Neuro Linguistic Programming offers individuals a structured approach to release and relinquish unproductive behaviors, beliefs, and value systems that hinder the attainment of success. This is accomplished through the establishment of a structured framework that facilitates the emergence of novel behaviors, beliefs, and value systems, ultimately leading to increased productivity and the attainment of individual objectives.

Commencement of the Framework for Neuro Linguistic Programming

In light of this framework, it is imperative to establish individualized expectations, boundaries, limitations, and regulations pertaining to the utilization of Neuro Linguistic Programming methods. By doing so, one can preemptively avert any potential misinterpretation of these techniques in the future, thereby mitigating the risks of personal frustrations and, on occasion, even delusional states. Put simply, it is essential to have a clear understanding of your desired outcomes and your level of adaptability before delving into the study of NLP strategies and techniques.

Neuro Linguistic Programming State
In order to fully leverage the principles and strategies of Neuro Linguistic Programming, it is imperative that one is adequately prepared on all fronts - physically, emotionally, and mentally. This is due to the fact that there will be occasions where the utilization of NLP techniques will necessitate the execution of the subsequent actions:

Recall poignant emotional experiences within your thoughts, encompassing feelings of joy, exhilaration, euphoria, sorrow, and bereavement, among others. Modification of certain physiological behaviors such as hand movements, individual posture, and gait patterns; Engaging in the process of addressing and seeking to amend detrimental beliefs impeding personal well-being.

Neuro Linguistic Programming Outcome Frequently, the objectives pertaining to your professional endeavors tend to diverge, clash, or be incompatible with the objectives you desire for your relationships, family, and personal life on one hand, and your health and well-being on the other. If these objectives are successfully attained, it will contribute to the development of a well-rounded individual such as yourself. The patterns, techniques, and strategies of

Neuro Linguistic Programming can assist you in aligning your aspirations in terms of physical and financial well-being, as well as personal relationships, both individually and within your family, to form a cohesive and unified objective. The preferred terminology for this concept is the desired state, which will be explored extensively in chapter 4.

Neuro Linguistic Programming Rapport
Neuro Linguistic Programming Rapport pertains to the establishment of a seamless and meaningful exchange of information and understanding among two or more individuals. There exist two distinct modalities of leveraging rapport for the fulfillment of personal objectives. These are the:
State of rapport; and
Break of rapport.
To put it succinctly, the utilization of a state of rapport is employed when one

desires to establish a connection with, exert influence over, or be susceptible to being influenced by a specific individual or collective entity. Conversely, the utilization of a break of rapport allows for the deliberate disconnection, lack of influence, or avoidance of a specific individual or group.

Practical Implementation: Utilization of Matching and Mirroring NLP Technique

If one desires to establish a connection with, exert influence upon, or be influenced by a specific individual, a conscious choice can be made to align one's own behavior, body language, hand gestures, language characteristics, and body postures with those of that person. This will signal to the individual with whom you are engaging in dialogue that you are undertaking a comprehensive and meaningful discussion. Consequently, an individual will experience a heightened sense of affinity towards you.

However, should you wish to refrain from establishing a connection, exerting influence, or being influenced by an individual, you can deliberately abstain from imitating their conduct, physical movements, manual gestures, linguistic patterns, and bodily stance.

Current Strategy

The present approach carries both advantages and disadvantages. Firstly, it is important to acknowledge that the current strategy pertains to the various elements, endeavors, and conduct that one deliberately carries out with the objective of attaining their genuine aspirations. Conversely, the concept of current strategy also encompasses the deliberate execution of actions, conduct, and behavior that impede the achievement of one's objectives.

Technique or Task
This pertains to the instrumental resources that Neuro Linguistic Programming will furnish to attain the intended state or outcome. Techniques or Tasks pertain to all internal and external assets and provisions that...
It is imperative that you attain the state or outcome you desire; and
You have right now

Future Pace
Envisioning the future is an exercise that calls upon the power of your imagination. In precise terms, future pacing entails an exercise that prompts the cultivation of one's imaginative faculties to establish a comprehensive connection between their current state and the envisioned state or desired outcome. This will allow you to establish a rapport with your current assets and

learn how to leverage these resources to achieve your intended outcome.

Conclude the Neuro Linguistic Programming Framework

This pertains to the framework in which you have already determined the desired state or outcome, while considering your personal expectations, boundaries, limitations, and rules that were established within the initial framework of Neuro Linguistic Programming. This will enhance your confidence in adopting NLP techniques and strategies, as it strengthens the positive aspects you have derived from employing them. This will enhance your propensity to employ the techniques and strategies of NLP in subsequent instances, thereby actualizing your desired state.

Mind Governance: Who Provides Guidance In Shaping Your Thoughts?

Suppose you were to enter a taxi and politely instruct the driver to refrain from transporting you to a specific destination. It may appear peculiar, but quite often this is the reality of our existence.

The main focus of this chapter will be to thoroughly examine the coherence of our actions and gain clarity on our intended direction.

Within the realm of natural language processing (NLP), lies the concept of the results framework, wherein the components integral to valuable objectives are examined and harnessed to optimize the likelihood of attaining our desired outcomes.

Let us endeavor to enhance our cognitive mastery and discern the true guiding forces within us.

Articulate your objective. What is your intended destination?

Within the field of NLP, it is postulated that all individuals possess innate capabilities that can be harnessed, necessitating the identification of suitable strategies or methods for their manifestation. If one is able to discover the appropriate path, they will attain fruitful outcomes and acquire confirmation that they are progressing towards the correct course.

This approach proves highly advantageous when employed towards your desired aims, particularly when seeking to implement significant transformations or when encountering obstacles in your progress. Additionally, it is invaluable for making nuanced modifications to existing goals or aspirations.

In order to accomplish this objective, it is imperative to inquire oneself essential queries:

What specific goals do you aim to accomplish?

In what specific location, at what particular time, in the company of whom, and under what set of circumstances do you seek to accomplish the intended outcome?

What factors impede your ability to already achieve that outcome?

What specific resources would be instrumental in facilitating the attainment of your objectives?

What methods will you employ to reach your destination and what initial measure will you take to accomplish this outcome?

What specific goals do you aspire to accomplish?

It is imperative to understand the issue, aspiration, or goal at hand. It is both positively formulated and subject to your control, ensuring clarity.

I prefer not to experience distress."

This does not pertain to an objective; rather, it embodies a statement. Similarly, the brain does not accurately process negative speech. To effect change in this matter, one should redirect their thoughts towards alternate considerations and subsequently contemplate:

Despite the potential influence of external factors such as a partner or boss on my emotional state, I am more likely to be persuasive when I maintain a sense of control."

Determine the point in time at which you will attain it.

Your objective is characterized by utmost sophistication; thus, it is imperative that you possess adequate substantiation. It is actively pursuing a pragmatic approach and implementing the requisite measures to attain it.

Did you specify a date?

By the end of the semester, I aspire to enhance my proficiency in the English language."

Where and with whom?

Every individual is actively engaged in the pursuit of personal goals, dedicating a significant portion of their lifetime towards this endeavor. However, upon achieving these ambitions, individuals often find themselves devoid of contentment, subsequently seeking out new objectives as the initial ones did not align with their true desires.

Allow me to provide an illustration: consider the scenario wherein, from a tender age, you have harbored a fervent aspiration to become a doctor. Given a steady exposure to depictions of distinguished medical professionals in their impeccably attired regalia through television and other media platforms, the seeds of this aspiration have taken root and blossomed into an enduring dream. In order to establish your commitment, you may consider embarking on a path such as volunteering for the Red Cross. This would allow you to gain firsthand experience in the field, enabling you to ascertain the reality of the profession and affirm your willingness to dedicate several years to pursuing a university degree that will undoubtedly shape your lifelong career.

What factors are impeding your progress in attaining the desired outcome?

There exists a dual inquiry herein, namely the enumeration of actionable points and the exploration of your thoughts and emotions.

When contemplating the factors impeding one's ability to appear persuasive, an individual may experience feelings of frustration due to the presence of restrictive thoughts that require diligent attention in order to be addressed effectively. Examine the elements of reality and discern the barriers that hinder the formulation of feasible strategies in order to accomplish objectives.

The necessary resources to assist in its creation.

This is categorized into two sections: firstly, the existing resources at your disposal, and secondly, the resources that are required. In the field of Natural Language Processing (NLP), resources encompass various elements such as knowledge, time, financial means, experiences, assistance, connections, and more.

Now you must analyze the resources at your disposal in order to enhance your persuasiveness.

It may be advantageous to employ a success narrative prior to commencing your discourse, as this can enhance your persuasiveness.

One must undertake an analysis of the requirements, ascertain the necessary resources, evaluate the existing assets, and determine the most effective approach for handling the given situation.

What is your plan for achieving the desired outcome?

Without the implementation of measures, the goal remains a mere concept; it is imperative to have a clear understanding of the responsible parties, specific tasks, methodologies, schedule, and locations within your domain.

In the field of natural language processing (NLP), the underlying principle is that possessing a greater range of alternatives is advantageous. The presence of a singular approach as a sole determinant of success within a plan is a harbinger of failure. A plan represents a singular pathway, whereas the inclusion of multiple alternative routes is imperative.

Mental Dichotomy: Alignment / Discrepancy

Undoubtedly, there have been instances in which you have experienced the simultaneous desire to both venture to a new location and to remain in your current surroundings. There exists within us an inherent conflict between the desire to engage in a certain action and the opposing inclination that discourages it.

This phenomenon can be described as incongruity, characterized by instances of perceived conflict in the pursuit of a desired outcome. This phenomenon occurs in various contexts, such as when one desires to venture into mountainous terrains or relax on coastal beaches.

When one finds oneself in an opportune moment, in which all components align seamlessly, this state is referred to as being in a state of utmost concentration or being in a state of uninterrupted flow. In the field of NLP, the term used is congruent. Being duly cognizant of your own indications of inconsistency grants you the ability to promptly discern conflict.

Inconsistency in beliefs or thoughts necessitates the expenditure of personal effort to conquer an aspect of oneself that resists pursuing a particular course of action. A significant portion of the psychological and physical strain occurs when the mind vigorously attempts to surpass the body's natural inclination to refrain from engaging in actions that compromise one's integrity.

One advantageous aspect is acquiring the ability to synchronize one's actions with guiding principles. This is the method employed to attain consensus regarding a desired outcome. Reflect upon the time in your early years when you earnestly desired a high-quality toy as a present, and ardently yearned for its acquisition. Over the course of your lifetime, you have encountered numerous parallel instances pertaining to something coveted, be it through literary works, cinematographic experiences, or interpersonal encounters.

The Fundamental Tenets Of Neuro-Linguistic Programming

In the field of NLP, certain fundamental concepts or presuppositions are designed to serve as the foundation upon which the application of **NLP** is based. They enable the utilization of **NLP** in accordance with its intended design. Natural Language Processing (NLP) is not simply a haphazard assortment of techniques aimed at executing tasks on behalf of others. This does not align with its intended purpose. Individuals who possess professional training in the field of **NLP** exhibit distinct usage patterns and possess a keen awareness of the limitations associated with it.

In this chapter, we will examine the fundamental principles of **NLP** that have prevailed since its inception. Incorporating these concepts into your understanding will enable you to effectively utilize NLP. Inauspicious notions or anticipations are not congruent with an idealistic outlook. In actuality, they demonstrate a proactive approach, providing explicit instructions on the utilization of **NLP** techniques. Failing to adhere to these guidelines can readily result in harm to other individuals. Please ensure that you take note of these basic principles of Natural Language Processing when carrying out the task.

The General Concepts

- Natural Language Processing (NLP) constitutes a framework rather than a conventional theory. In its essence, the analysis is subject to subjectivity. The experience is subject to variation for all individuals.

- Instead of perceiving **NLP** as a model focused on repairing, it should be regarded as a model that generates. This suggests that the focus of **NLP** is not on the investigation or assessment of the underlying factors resulting in a problem, but rather on the identification and implementation of remedies for the challenges at hand. In the field of natural language processing (NLP), the practice involves incorporating additional choices rather than stripping them away.

• The mind and the body constitute a single entity.

• Each feature of human behavior can be ascribed to a system. • A system can be ascribed to every aspect of human behavior. • Each aspect of human behavior may be ascribed to a system.

• Your outward behavior may be influenced by the manner in which you employ your symbolic frameworks.

• If an action is within the capability of one person, it is theoretically attainable by any person.

• The cognitive capacity of the conscious mind is limited. • The conscious mind possesses a negligible level of ability. • The conscious mind exhibits minimal prowess. • The capacity for conscious thought is circumscribed.

Social Interaction

- It is incumbent upon you to acknowledge and assume accountability for the reaction elicited from others.
- It is essential that you accept the consequences of the feedback received from others.
- It falls within your purview to take ownership of the response evoked from others.
- It is crucial that you bear the responsibility for the reaction you elicit from others.

- Irrespective of individuals' current level of awareness, one must conduct themselves as though they possess the requisite mental support at all times.

To exert influence upon others, it is imperative that you initially perceive the world through your distinctive lens. In order to exert an influence upon them, one must initially strive to uncover their perspectives of the world and subsequently align with them accordingly.

- Individuals, equipped with the resources at their disposal or those they perceive to possess, consistently arrive at judicious choices in any given circumstance.

• It is imperative to comprehend that each individual's perception of truth is unique and varied. Individuals may possess divergent perspectives on truth, all of which hold equal validity and deviate from your own. Each of these entities serves as distinct depictions of reality, akin to cartographic renderings of separate landscapes detached from the actual physical terrain.

• Individuals will continue to respond to their subjective understanding of truth, taking into account not only their sensory experiences but also their internal perceptions.

Personal Development

• The individual who possesses the highest level of behavioral adaptability enjoys the most substantial advantage. • The individual exhibiting the utmost versatility in their behavior attains the most prominent advantage. • The person who demonstrates the greatest capacity for versatile behavior reaps the most noteworthy benefit. • The individual with the most extensive range of behavioral flexibility gains the most significant advantage. The individual in question could potentially exert the greatest influence on the outcome. Consequently, it is imperative that both your conduct and attitude demonstrate an enhanced level of adaptability.

- Remind yourself that there exists a resolution for every challenge. - Convince yourself that a viable solution can be found for any issue. - Assure yourself that there is always a remedy for every problem.

• It is imperative to discern an individual's personality and self-perception from their conduct.

• In the life of any individual, it can be assumed that every action or act is characterized by positive intentions, albeit to some degree.

- If the current approach is not yielding desired results, regard it as constructive feedback and consistently enhance your strategy.

Please be informed that these ideals should not be regarded as absolute truths or factual assertions. Instead, we consider any truth in **NLP** to be a tentative proposition. There may arise situations in which the rules will not be applicable, and such occurrences are deemed acceptable. The key lies in consistently upholding the validity of the values. While certain ideas might appear implausible, adopting an approach that treats them as valid enables us to constantly adapt our means of communication until we reach our objective or recognize the other party's lack of openness.

Rapport

The fundamental principles of **NLP** are comprised of four pillars: collaboration, heightened sensory perception or awareness, logical analysis based on outcomes or performance, and adaptability in behavior. These fundamental principles constitute the very basis of the **NLP** theory, and they validate all the findings derived from the NLP. It is imperative to prioritize these concepts during interactions as they are instrumental in effecting transformative change in individuals' lives. These foundations can potentially mitigate or eliminate occurrences of miscommunication, thus facilitating the enhancement of mutual understanding. In a particular chapter, commencing with the article, each of the four pillars are duly examined.

The Bestowal of Interpersonal Connection

In order to establish social bonds, individuals engage in mutual connections. In the realm of cultivating interpersonal connections, the **NLP** approach offers individuals a pivotal and noteworthy benefit, namely. The overwhelming majority of individuals engage in driving in the fast lane within the current cultural context. One of the fundamental principles of **NLP** involves recognizing and acknowledging the fast-paced lifestyles that individuals lead, consequently imparting a crucial lesson in politely declining requests or favors that would further burden an already hectic schedule. However, it is imperative to ensure that such declinations are made honestly and effectively, with the ultimate goal of maintaining and nurturing both personal and professional relationships. This phenomenon is referred to as a partnership, which involves acquiring the skills to establish connections and, when necessary, handling the aspect of terminating specific relationships.

NLP suggests that by fostering substantial connections with individuals through interaction, one can attain success. It is imperative, at this juncture, to acknowledge that cultivating a strong self-connection serves as a catalyst for achievement in NLP. Consider revising the sentence in a more formal tone as follows: "Taking into consideration one of the foundational assumptions of NLP, it is believed that the true essence of communication lies in the response received, disregarding the underlying intent behind such communication. To rephrase this in a more concise manner, the pivotal aspect of interaction between the sender and the receiver hinges upon the reaction elicited by the former." Taking this assumption into account, the potential elucidation would be a deficiency in connection, stemming from ambiguity or opposition towards a specific interaction.

The aim of fostering or creating alliances with all that is mutually shared is never a comprehensive accord. However, it would be more beneficial for the partnership to facilitate the comprehension of the message by the other party. Establishing rapport enables individuals to effectively communicate their message. The report should aim to ensure clear comprehension for another individual regarding your choice of using the term "blue." A report is characterized by the capacity to engage in meaningful communication with another individual or a collective, established on shared comprehension, trust, and consistency derived from the preceding discussion.

The Advantages of Establishing Rapport

The advantages of cultivating connections with influential individuals in your personal sphere and within your broader social network can be encapsulated by the Five Rs:

- Retrieval: Developing robust connections facilitates enhanced memorability of your persona. When you make a favorable impression on someone during your initial encounter or introduction, it remains ingrained in their memory.

- Acknowledgment: An individual who possesses strong interpersonal relationships has an impact on every individual they come across. The first impression endures. It is important to be aware that there is no possibility of having a second chance to create an initial impact. Please take note of the details of your initial encounter.

- Response: Following the initial introduction, there is a sense of exhilaration that arises when one is able to elicit a favorable response from an individual during subsequent interactions.

- Esteem: A prosperous relationship provides an opportunity to earn the respect of others. You have gained the trust and confidence of others. You develop a heightened understanding of the ways in which you engage in collective work and provide assistance to individuals.

Responsibility: Although it is indeed possible to forge a positive connection between individuals through the demonstration of good relations, it is ultimately the duty of successful individuals to proactively foster relationships with others. It is advisable to follow this practice in all partnerships. The individual who assumes primary responsibility for cultivating or enhancing relationships is the one who assumes leadership within the relationship.

Rapport Building Strategies

One can acquire the skills and cultivate proficiency in utilizing **NLP** for the purpose of fostering interpersonal connections. Contrasting with the realms of chemistry or biology, where knowledge and skills can be obtained through experimentation in controlled laboratory settings, the refinement of relationships occurs through active engagement and interaction with individuals in the social sphere, such as those with whom you coexist and collaborate. In the field of Natural Language Processing (NLP), the strategies encompass essential competencies and additional refined methodologies. The following sections elaborate upon several prominent approaches for cultivating connections with individuals.

When establishing a connection, the primary abilities required include:

• Seeking information

• Active listening • Attentive listening • Engaged listening • Discerning listening • Comprehending listening

• Structuring and coordination

• Conducting scholarly inquiry. • Engaging in investigative study. • Pursuing academic investigation.

Develop a resilient and inquisitive disposition towards fellow individuals. Being actively engaged in the lives of others emanates a sense of empathy. It is common for individuals to perceive the genuine concern and attention conveyed when one demonstrates genuine interest in them. For instance, endeavor to ascertain the most optimal method of engaging with an individual through a systematic examination, utilizing an analytical methodology, in the circumstance where a formal introduction has not been made. Regardless of the methodology employed, it is imperative to accurately convey your intended objective. An effective approach to initiate a conversation is to discuss topics of significance. Please make a conscious effort to carefully attend to the response(s) provided in response to your intentional inquiry.

Remain vigilant and actively seek out prospects for fostering relationship growth. If you believe it is necessary, provide aid. Through the application of relationships in the workplace or industry using NLP, collaborations may assume a more partnership-oriented nature rather than relying solely on friendship. Please be assured that **NLP** is universally applicable across all conditions and domains of human interest.

The report encompasses the capacity to perceive and engage with fellow individuals who share a common wavelength. In actuality, a substantial portion of how individuals perceive your genuineness during interactions is not predicated on the verbatim dialogue, but rather on the manner in which it is articulated with regards to:

• Facial expression; "• Visage; "• Countenance; "• Aspect.

• Hand movement(s); • Non-verbal cue(s); • Physical indication(s); • Action(s) displayed through the body or limbs; • Motion(s) made with the hands or body.

• Body alignment;

• Pitch of voice, etc.

Matching & Mirroring

This is the juncture at which the neuro aspect of **NLP** becomes relevant. Matching and mirroring is regarded as one of the most effective strategies for establishing relationships in the field of neuroscience. According to experts, matching and mirroring are mechanisms by which an individual can develop a heightened sensitivity to another individual's cognitive and perceptual framework. The auditory perception through the use of one's ears is the customary mode of assimilating spoken language. In the field of Natural Language Processing (NLP), employing techniques such as matching and mirroring allows individuals to engage in listening with their entire physique, rather than solely relying on auditory perception.

It is noteworthy that individuals naturally engage in simple mirroring during the formation of relationships. Nevertheless, when it comes to the fields of **NLP** and basic imitation, it is imperative to be mindful of the nuanced distinction that exists between synchronizing one's movements with another individual. Individuals will invariably be aware when you indulge in mockery towards them.

According to the principles of the **NLP** approach, it is advisable for an individual seeking to form a connection with another person to consider the following factors and strive for equilibrium:

- Posture and nonverbal cues; • Alignment and physical movements; • Body language and positioning; • Pose and bodily signals; • Stance and nonverbal expressions; • Attitude and gestures; • Bearing and corporal indicators.

- Respiratory rate;

- The cadence of motion and levels of vitality; and

- Tone of voice and cadence of speech.

Several Activities for Establishing Rapport

In this particular foundation of NLP, the subsequent reporting exercises will contribute to the augmentation of your proficiency:

Exercise Number 1

Seek out an individual who is not particularly familiar to you. Initiate a dialogue and engage in the emulation of his or her bodily position and gestures in the presence of that individual. Ensure that you refrain from encountering any consequences as a result of being discovered. Prior to emulating the pose and posture, it is crucial to observe a brief interval of approximately 5 seconds following the individual's action. In order to enhance your personal security in the event of encountering difficulties, it is advisable to carry a duplicate of this eBook and elucidate the designated task within the academic setting.

This exercise involves the utilization of a solitary missile to engage two jet fighters, thus providing an opportunity to enhance both your proficiency in mirroring and your ability to effectively communicate within a relationship-oriented framework.

Exercise Number 2

Once you have completed the aforementioned exercise several times, proceed to engage in this activity until you are content that you have established a rapport with your "unassuming" exercise companions. Seek out an individual with whom you possess limited familiarity, yet approach this encounter with the conviction that you and said individual share a preexisting connection and rapport in the present context. In this exercise, the premise is that you possess significant familiarity with this individual, and it is anticipated that you will interact seamlessly.

In your initial endeavor, there is a possibility of either success or failure, yet through perseverance, you will inevitably comprehend the potency of establishing rapport. Do not perceive this practice as an endeavor to manipulate individuals. If you demonstrate exceptional proficiency in this task, there exists a substantial likelihood that you will be able to effectively enhance your life with the application of NLP. There is no justification for why one cannot cultivate a relationship with oneself as a means to foster relationships with others. In order to motivate yourself to become the change you desire, employ such self-constancy.

Sensory Acuity

How can individuals ascertain whether they possess the requisite sensory acuteness or sensitivity level necessary to attain their objectives of life transformation? All individuals possess an innate awareness and concern for environmental preservation. It is discernible whether an individual with whom you are conversing claims to be alright, despite the fact that they are truly not. You would likely have observed the unmistakable ambiance when visiting a friend's residence, which encompasses not only discernible visual cues such as the color palette, artful architecture, and meticulously crafted surroundings but also the unique olfactory and auditory elements. You are currently demonstrating exceptional sensory acuity in your workplace.

Sensory acuity or perception constitutes the second tenet of NLP. Sensory acuity refers to the capacity to perceptively discern and differentiate the diverse manifestations of sensory stimuli emanating from the surrounding environment. The capacity to understand and perceive information conveyed by the senses, and utilize that understanding to generate user input or response, is tantamount to the human ability to acquire or discern such sensory data. On this celestial body, the perceptual acuity that sustains individuals tends to be inadequately developed. Could you envision the remarkable potency that individuals could potentially harness if the sharpness of their sensory faculties were heightened? Cease to envision this scenario any longer, as NLP will optimize SA and facilitate the desired transformation.

The Mental Computer

Upon one's entrance into this world, one is bestowed with a physical form complete with bodily components such as organs and blood, as well as the faculties of senses, muscles, and bones. The aforementioned elegant apparatus functions harmoniously as a result of the cerebral capabilities endowed to every individual, serving as a masterful instrument of regulation and manipulation.

During the initial stages of life, the brain undergoes a complex process of establishing neural connections and arranging its systems. It requires several months for one to acquire the ability to manipulate their limbs effectively, as well as learn the fundamental skill of nourishing oneself. There is a temporal process involved when acquiring the ability to crawl, and subsequently walk, articulate sounds, develop communication skills, and even during the period when language has not yet been acquired.

Since our birth, we are continuously acquiring knowledge. We are acquiring the knowledge and skills necessary to navigate the intricacies of human existence, both through conscious and subconscious means. By adulthood, our brains possess a vast number of neurons, totaling billions in quantity, with each individual neuron boasting an impressive count of trillions of connections. These connections exhibit rapid transmission of information, akin to the speed of lightning traveling at a velocity of 250 miles per hour.

We are electrical. Similar to a computer system, we accumulate and retain information by means of these connections, encompassing our sensory perceptions, recollections, emotions, and cognitive processes. With our eyes either open or closed, our internal computer possesses the capability to render visual representations of images from both the past and the present. There exists no constraint on the extent to which our brains can retain and store information. In contrast to computers, which possess finite storage capacity, the human brain is believed to possess an inexhaustible capacity for storing information throughout our lifetimes. It serves as the operational hub that governs our overall functionality.

The brain exhibits plasticity, thereby suggesting its capacity for transformation. Similar to the pliability of a muscle, the mind possesses the capacity to be molded; yet, in the absence of mental exercise, it can become entrenched in stagnant patterns of thinking that obstruct personal development. Engaging in continuous mental exercise, acquiring new knowledge, enhancing memory, and forging fresh neural pathways or reinforcing established, favorable connections, expands one's capacity to experience life more profoundly, optimistically, and receptively, thereby encompassing the various opportunities presented by the world.

Having a comprehension of the functioning of your brain plays a pivotal role in comprehending the potential benefits that Neuro-Linguistic Programming can offer to you. How we perceive and assimilate information influences our capacity to learn from personal encounters and shape our self-perception and belief system.

Reality encompasses all elements that exist beyond one's own self: fellow individuals, the entirety of the terrestrial realm, the cosmos, and the vast expanse of the universe. The human brain possesses the capacity to assimilate two million units of information per second. However, the quantity of data or input we actually perceive is significantly lower, owing to the manner in which we process our experiences.

Through our senses, we construct our own perception or representation, known as a map, of the external reality that exists beyond ourselves. As a consequence, we inadvertently eliminate, manipulate, and oversimplify the fragments of data that we can perceive, resulting in a reduction from two million to approximately 133,000 pieces of information. We craft our personal narrative of the world, selectively filtering out information that conflicts with our internal discourse, presumptions, and subjective convictions. Consequently, we instinctively gauge our surroundings based on our individual comprehension, recollections, past experiences, and unique disposition.

We establish the significance of something by constructing our perception of reality based on our personal encounters and self-awareness, thereby attributing meaning and value to every experience. Without comprehending its significance, we are unable to formulate our thoughts or respond appropriately.

This connotation gives rise to a sentiment or mental condition, prompting a reaction or behavior. When an individual describes something as frightening, it is due to the cognitive evaluation conducted by their mind, which relies on past encounters to determine the fear-inducing nature of that particular thing. Should you choose to alter your perspective, it is within your prerogative to determine that it lacks elements that instill fear. The reason for its existence is solely due to your assertion. The reason for this is the manner in which you articulate it.

Integration Of Parts

This approach is widely utilized and featured prominently in NLP workshops and literature. The premise of this theory is rooted in the notion that internal conflicts arise when contemplating actions. The aspect concerning "parts" is in the realm of metaphor, yet it serves as a practical and readily comprehensible metaphor. In situations of inner conflict, it is common to express our hesitation by stating, "I am torn between two desires – one part of me is inclined towards this course of action, while another part is against it." It is possible to conceive all our behaviors or actions as existing on a spectrum. On one hand, there exists a complete alignment. Actions that exhibit complete congruency are effortlessly executed and intuitively inherent. There exists no internal opposition. For instance, consider a scenario where you are strolling along the path and happen to notice a $10 bill resting on the pavement. In such a situation, it would be highly appropriate for you to demonstrate congruence by inclining towards the ground and retrieving it. Perhaps, prior to leaning over, it would be advisable to promptly verify whether someone inadvertently dropped it. However, upon acknowledging the absence of any witnesses, the possession of the money becomes rightfully yours, and stooping down to retrieve it can be undertaken with utmost assurance and assurance. An alternative scenario arises when one experiences ennui during a leisurely Saturday afternoon. You have sent messages to several acquaintances and are casually browsing through various television channels. Upon the occurrence of a vibrational alert from your mobile device, you promptly incline towards it and acquire it with utmost consistency and conformity. Take into account an alternative scenario displaying significantly lower congruity. You find yourself in the solitude of your residence on a Tuesday evening. It's past ten. A resounding knock can be heard emanating from the entrance. It's unexpected. Contrast the manner in which you would arise and respond to a situation like that with how you would act if you were anticipating the arrival of a close acquaintance. With regard to a familiar acquaintance, one might enthusiastically exclaim, "The door is unlocked!" However, when faced with an unfamiliar and forceful knocking during the late hours, one would cautiously approach the entrance and meticulously inspect the peephole in order to ascertain the identity of the visitor. Achieving congruence becomes a simple task when we possess a comprehensive understanding of all the variables involved and exhibit a fearless disposition towards any potential negative consequences. However, in situations where the outcome of our endeavors remains uncertain, achieving congruence becomes a challenging endeavor. In each of these instances, we are addressing an external occurrence. However, engaging in behavior or contemplating behavior from an incongruous perspective can cause significant impairment. Once we dip below a certain threshold of congruence, a sense of stagnation ensues. When contemplating the approach of engaging in a conversation with an individual while traversing the room, it behooves one to consider the potential repercussions, both favorable and adverse, that may arise. It would be greatly appreciated if you were to proceed towards that direction and engage in a captivating dialogue, leading to the establishment of a remarkable relationship, which would be truly commendable. However, in the event that you were to approach that location and face public rejection, it would be observed by everyone present, thereby necessitating your return home in a defeated manner. That would absolutely suck. The integration of components will prove beneficial in this particular domain. A portion of your being harbours the desire to approach, while another portion is engulfed by a sense of trepidation.

Negotiations

The process of integrating various components bears resemblance to a diplomatic dialogue between two parties. Both parties are striving to secure the most favorable agreement achievable. Thus, they deliberate intensively until a consensus is achieved that meets the expectations of all parties involved. This may appear dissimilar to the situation of contemplating walking across the room. Ultimately, the shared objective of the star baseball player and his agent engaging in negotiations with the team owner remains constant. The purpose of the negotiation is to establish mutually acceptable terms. However, the two components of your being appear to be moving in seemingly contradictory directions. There is a desire for you to remain in your current location, yet another desire exists to move towards that area. In what manner can we engage in a process of negotiation between two entities, even if they are metaphorical counterparts, given their apparent inclination towards divergent objectives?

Elevate your cognitive perspective.

This is the ideal environment for fostering creative thinking. The initial measure involves acknowledging the constituent elements as autonomous entities possessing their own volition and motives. The key is to engage in dialogue with each component, progressively ascending to more elevated levels of requirements, until we achieve concurrence. What constitute higher-level criteria? Assume that you desire sustenance. Consuming food is the fundamental criterion. The criteria at a more advanced level are in addition to those. The preferred culinary option you wish to partake in. The kind of establishment in which you would prefer to dine. And what is your reason for desiring to dine at such an establishment? Perhaps you desire pizza due to the serene ambiance, affordable rates, and extensive selection of games that your nearby pizzeria offers. They also employ waitstaff that is adorably charming. If you happen to find yourself in the company of a cohort, whereupon certain individuals express their desire for cheeseburgers, you may proceed to employ the identical methodology. What else holds significance in relation to consumption? What type of dining ambiance holds significance for them? If one continues to progress through increasingly higher levels of abstraction, it is plausible to ascertain consensus among individuals with regard to their willingness to dine at a particular establishment, so long as the establishment offers televised games and employs aesthetically pleasing servers. "It is possible that the real food (pizza vs. The significance of cheeseburgers, and similar items, pales in comparison to that of the environment. We will proceed with the identical course of action for your individual components. At this juncture, consensus is assured. All the components are ultimately performing activities to bolster and cater to your needs. The key lies in ascending to higher meta levels of criteria in order to reach a consensus. Let us hypothetically examine the aspect of your being that displays a inclination to remain comfortably in your current state, unwilling to venture into the realm of potential rejection. Let us envisage a dialogue with the entity.

What course of action would you like to pursue?

I desire to remain in this location.

What is the reason behind your desire to pursue such a course of action?

Due to the potential risk of facing repercussions, it is advisable not to proceed to that location.

What kind of trouble?

We might get rejected.

I see. What would be the potential outcome if our proposal were to be declined?

Everybody would see.

OK. What would that mean?

That implication suggests that no one in this vicinity would engage in conversation with us.

I see. And would that be considered undesirable?

Indeed, such an outcome would be unfavorable.

What negative implications might arise from this situation?

Due to the absence of companionship, solitude would ensue.

Do you find solace in solitude?

No.

Do you find solace in the presence of others?

Yes.

However, on the condition that it is deemed safe.

Correct.

To ensure clarity, may I ascertain that companionship and safety hold significance in your perspective?

Certainly, it would be greatly appreciated if we could acquire those two items.

Cool.

Now we have gained an understanding of the desires of those components. It is imperative that we engage in a conversation with the counterpart. We engage in dialogue with our hypothetical alternative persona, envisioning the potential responses it might provide.

Hey.

Hey.

Do you intend to approach her by foot and engage in conversation?

Yep.

What is the reason for your desire to engage in such an action?

Dude, seriously? Observe her! She possesses an endearing quality and has kindly bestowed upon us two smiles already.

I comprehend, thus you have a fondness for engaging in conversation with attractive young women?

What, are you slow? Indeed, I derive enjoyment from engaging in conversations with individuals of a feminine persuasion who possess appealing and endearing qualities.

Please oblige my curiosity, what is it that attracts you to engaging in conversations with appealing young women?

Ascertaining mutual interest is crucial, as it has the potential to foster a potential connection and enable us to convene.

I see. Thus, it appears that you are contemplating the possibility of pursuing a romantic commitment?

Yes. Assuming she possesses an agreeable disposition.

Indeed, if she possesses a commendable character and exhibits affinity towards us, engaging in a relationship with her would prove advantageous.

Indeed, it would be quite favorable to be in the company of an aesthetically pleasing young woman who possesses an agreeable disposition.

May I inquire as to the rationale behind this?

It has come to my attention that humans generally derive satisfaction from engaging in social interactions with their fellow beings.

I see. Is it not to your satisfaction to be alone?

No, I would prefer to spend time with an attractive woman who genuinely appreciates me.

Indeed, that is the reason you have expressed an interest in proceeding on foot to that location.

Indeed, in order to ascertain our compatibility.

And if we click?

Subsequently, we can enjoy pleasant moments in each other's company.

Right, thanks.

After engaging in discussions with both parties, it is now incumbent upon us to facilitate a mutually agreeable resolution that addresses the respective needs of both sides. Typically, the standard procedure involves engaging in a comprehensive dialogue with every individual. You initially inquire if they are available to engage in conversation outside. Please take a seat and extend your hands, with your palms facing upward. You strive to generate a comprehensive and intricate mental depiction of each component to the fullest extent possible. Conceive of it as if it were an integral aspect of your being, one that is perceptible through sight, sound, smell, and touch. Observe every component with its individual set of distinct aspirations and concerns. Carefully engage in a conversation with each component, gradually identifying commonalities between their respective goals. Typically, this is where the conclusion takes place. During NLP seminars, participants are advised to engage in the exercise of envisioning the two distinct components engaging in a dialogue, subsequently facilitating an amalgamation of the two into a unified "super part" to ensure harmony and resolution. However, it has been observed that the integration of these techniques into one's neurology typically requires a substantial amount of time.

Maintain the Separation of Components.

A viable approach would entail retaining the individual components as distinct entities while ensuring that each part fulfills the highest standards of safety and companionship, for the purposes of our illustration, and utilizing them as available resources. Regard them as figments of one's imagination. They are both employed under your supervision.

They both share a common desire for your well-being. It is important to acknowledge that an increase in conflict leads to a proportional increase in the duration required for identifying a resolution. Making the choice between consuming cheeseburgers or pizza is a straightforward decision. Initiating conversations with individuals who are visually appealing is not recommended. Take into account that the initial step merely encompasses the identification and extraction of the distinct elements, followed by obtaining their respective perspectives. After recognizing the two components associated with any conflicting desire, typically entailing financial or social security, allocate sufficient time for them to engage in creativity. Envision their presence when you encounter such scenarios. Envision that both individuals possess the ability to impart guidance to you. Envision a scenario wherein individuals from the Research and Development department engage in frequent debates and conflicts with their counterparts from the

Accounting department during company meetings. Both individuals share a common desire to enhance the welfare of the organization, albeit employing disparate approaches to achieve this goal. Ultimately, however, prosperous organizations ascertain methods to reach consensus. Consider conceptualizing your individual components as distinct elements within your "internal divisions." Avoid imposing undue pressure on them to reach a consensus, allow them sufficient time to resolve any conflicts. Convene weekly meetings with them and envision them engaging in deliberation over the optimal course of action. Take notes. Be creative.

NLP And Self Talk

It is a commonplace occurrence for individuals to engage in soliloquy. In what manner do you engage in self-dialogue, manifesting either positivity or negativity? Although engaging in positive self-dialogue can enhance the quality of one's life, indulging in negative self-dialogue has the potential to drastically disrupt one's overall well-being.

Negative self-talk entails engaging in an unfavorable mode of self-communication characterized by a pessimistic, imperative, and unduly judgmental approach. Engaging in detrimental self-talk manifests when utterances like, "Why are you so unintelligent?!" or "You have consistently failed to accomplish anything correctly!" emerge from your inner dialogue.

Effectively Confronting and Overcoming Negative Internal Dialogue

The inner voice within oneself generates visual representations. These images have the potential to either facilitate or hinder one's progress in life. By eliminating or at least endeavoring to diminish negative self-dialogue, one can commence utilizing the subconscious mind to construct positive visualizations that will propel one towards achieving success.

Transform your use of negative self-dialogue by implementing the subsequent measures:

Step 1: Reduce the intensity of your self-critical inner dialogue until it completely dissipates. Now replace those negative thoughts with positive affirmations.

A prime illustration would be when you find yourself uttering, "Why do you consistently commit foolish errors?" In such a situation, a more appropriate response would entail saying, "Very well, I shall utilize this as a point of reference and glean from this blunder in order to perform more admirably in the future." Alternatively, one might convey, "I perpetually acquire knowledge and enhance myself through previous errors."

Step 2: Alter the velocity of your pessimistic inner discourse to attenuate its high tempo. Altering the velocity renders it devoid of purpose. Once more, replace your negative internal dialogue with positive affirmations.

Thirdly, alter the tone of your negative self-dialogue to a comical rendition reminiscent of a cartoon character.

Step 4: Constrain the voice within an enclosed receptacle or container to prevent its leakage. Cover it thoroughly with padding to muffle the sound completely. Now, once more, replace that negative self-dialogue with positive self-affirmations.

Engaging in intrapersonal dialogue can be entrancing and enduring. Maintain a straightforward approach and persevere in your efforts.

What Capabilities Does Neurolinguistic Programming Possess And What Are Its Limitations?

Although the fundamental method of neuro-linguistic programming is derived from studying the speech patterns of highly accomplished and renowned therapists, it is not regarded as a variant of therapy.

NLP finds extensive applications in life counseling, executive coaching, and as a valuable tool for fostering goal-oriented communication in executive settings. consequently, NLP can be found within

- Sales seminars for sales promotion
- Professional development workshops focused on optimizing personnel management
- Seminars on the effective management of conflicts

- Psychosocial guidance
- Workshops on enhancing individual growth and self-improvement

The individuals who utilize NLP are also referred to as Practitioners. They assert that NLP is not a purely manipulative technique. Instead, they signify the notion that neuro-linguistic programming predominantly aims to enhance communication on both external and internal levels. It solely adheres to an individual's personal values and moral principles, and must align with the prevailing environmental context. The instrument known as the "Eco-Check" serves as a means to achieve this objective. The alterations instigated by neuro-linguistic programming ought to exclusively proceed in the intended trajectory.

"Future-Pace" refers to the alignment of actions with an individual's desires and objectives, encompassing the process of visualizing their aspirations and cultivating mental representations thereof. By doing so, a distinct influence is exerted on the act of breaking free from unfavorable thought and behavioral patterns and redirecting one's focus towards constructive thoughts and actions.

Neuro-linguistic programming cannot sufficiently replace the therapeutic benefits derived from depth psychological therapy, specifically in addressing and resolving traumatic experiences. Furthermore, the utilization of NLP for the purpose of exerting control over another individual's mind is highly ill-advised and should be strictly discouraged. Instead, NLP strives to acknowledge and enhance self-perception and the perception of others, specifically referring to one's own image and the image others hold, with the intention of refining and conveying it effectively and clearly through both spoken and non-verbal means. This also encompasses the embodiment of the solution and resource-centered frameworks of action and cognitive processes. The utilization of linguistic programming is employed in

- Business,
- Healthcare,
- Pedagogy
- Jurisdiction

Within the realm of business, NLP provides an expansive and bountiful domain for implementation, as it confers advantages to every facet of a commercial undertaking. Hence, neuro-linguistic programming serves as a fundamental framework for establishing effective communication within the context of proficient management.

Through the application of Natural Language Processing (NLP), it is possible to develop a mission statement and distinctive selling propositions by effectively determining and aligning corporate values and objectives. Concurrently, these aspects become increasingly explicit and conspicuous. NLP plays a crucial role in fostering a robust corporate culture within the employed workforce. The development of personnel and management of human resources predominantly depend on core principles of internal and external communication within the organization. The primary domain of utilization for NLP lies within the sales sector. This facilitates the successful execution of management objectives pertaining to sales by employees. Staff members acquire valuable insights and knowledge, thereby enhancing their ability to conduct sales presentations and customer consultations with greater ease.

Enhancement of customer satisfaction consequently results in the attainment of additional contractual agreements. Hence, it is not implausible to leverage

NLP in order to facilitate succession planning, company mergers, and analogous critical contract resolutions, thus ensuring seamless and satisfactory outcomes for all parties involved.

Foundations Of Neuro-Linguistic Programming

When Bandler and Grinder undertook the modeling of communication processes exhibited by exceptionally accomplished individuals, they encountered behavioral and cognitive patterns. These patterns were intentionally incorporated into the model of linguistic programming under the designation of "presuppositions." Fundamental premises underlying the conception of NLP are constituted by these presuppositions. The number of assumptions fluctuates based on the source employed. The subsequent assumptions provided are not exhaustive, but rather represent a selection of the ten most prevalent ones you will encounter.

The individual's subjective perspective, commonly referred to as one's worldview, does not necessarily align with objective reality or the actual topography of a given situation.

• The positive values remain unchanged. Conversely, the validity of the methods of behaviour may be called into question.

• Every action is motivated by a positive intention and bears a positive motive for the agent executing it.

• The received feedback pertaining to the communication holds significance.

• Communication is free from any deficiencies or inaccuracies. Once again, the feedback stands as the determining factor.

• Each behavior is derived from the specific context in which it serves a purpose.

All necessary resources have already been procured to facilitate the implementation of transformative measures.

- In the event that a particular course of action proves ineffective, it is advisable to consider an alternative approach.

The entity possessing the greatest range of behavioral possibilities retains dominion over a perpetual system.

In the event that an individual possesses the ability to accomplish a task, such behavior can be replicated and transmitted.

Anchoring refers to the fundamental technique employed in the field of neuro-linguistic programming.

The technique of anchoring holds utmost significance within the NLP model. It pertains to the correlation between a particular stimulus and the subsequent involuntary response that is either sought-after or not desired. The response is grounded in the process of conditioning. The aforementioned principle came to light by means of the researcher Iwan Pawlow, who executed experiments involving canines. The tolling of a bell elicited the secretion of saliva in the animals. By sounding the bell, he provided the stimulus associated with the availability of food.

By means of neuro-linguistic programming, these undesirable associations can be eradicated and substituted with new, desired ones. This method is commonly employed in the treatment of phobias to disengage the associations. The Fast Phobia Cure is employed to triumph over specific anxieties, while concurrently addressing any detrimental or undesirable behaviors, such as addiction or weight management.

Moreover, the method presents an additional potential application through the establishment of resource anchors combined with favorable and desired anchors. These purported resource anchors are connected to a stimulus that can be accessed at one's convenience.

Similarly, employing mild states of trance can be employed to enhance the practitioner's utilization of neuro-linguistic programming when applied to anchors.

4. New Behavior Generator

The 'New Behavior Generator' (BNG) is a highly effective strategy within the field of Neuro-Linguistic Programming (NLP) that facilitates the cultivation of novel characteristics, conduct, and routines, thereby enhancing one's self-esteem, happiness, tranquility, and accomplishments.

Guidelines for Implementing the Novel Behavior Generator Method

Allow me to provide you with the steps to effectively implement this strategy.

1. Locate a serene environment where you can engage in uninterrupted solitude for a duration of no less than 30 to 40 minutes. If you are cohabitating in the same room as someone else, kindly

request that individual refrain from disrupting your activities during a designated period. Please ensure you deactivate any loud household devices to avoid any potential interruptions during your practice of the technique.

2. Please recline or sit in a relaxed position either on the floor or your bed, while soothing your mind by recalling a pleasant memory.

3. Consider a person whom you regard as your role model, someone who serves as a source of inspiration and whom you aspire to emulate. Consider any aspect of that individual's conduct or practice that you would aspire to emulate. Take for example, the admiration you hold for your neighbor, a close confidant, whose unwavering dedication to their work captivates you. If you aspire to emulate such unwavering focus in your own life, consider adopting that commendable conduct.

4. Kindly, lower your eyelids and envision yourself observing a brief video excerpt of your neighbor diligently

engaged in their professional tasks. Observe her demeanor, mannerisms, posture, gait, verbal expressions, the content of her speech, as well as the various gestures she employs.

5. Consider whether that individual and their conduct elicit admiration from you. If you find yourself duly impressed, kindly proceed to the following stage. If not, consider an alternative person of your preference and commence the process from the initial stage.

6. If one finds a behavior that is admirable in a role model, and wishes to imitate it, one might consider placing oneself in the shoes of that inspiring individual and striving to conduct oneself in a similar manner. Adopt the perspective of that individual and introspect upon the experience of embodying their characteristics and demeanor.

7. Envision a prospective scenario wherein you aspire to emulate the conduct exhibited by the aforementioned individual. Continuously

envision that scenario and observe your subsequent conduct in that specific moment.

For instance, if you aspire to maintain unwavering focus on your tasks even amidst numerous distractions, envision yourself confronting and overcoming those impediments with determination and unwavering resolve.

8. Conduct a thorough examination of your approach towards overcoming these challenges. Continuously engage in self-observation for a period of time to facilitate a deeper comprehension of your recently developed conduct.

9. Embrace a more discerning perspective to reengage with actuality.

10. Reflect upon your actions during the time when you were striving to imitate your role model and comport yourself in a similar manner. Take note of your emotions and sensations when you engage in such behavior.

11. Whilst conducting oneself in such a manner, it is advisable to associate the

corresponding emotion with a hand gesture such as snapping one's fingers or applying pressure between the thumb and forefinger, or by employing any preferred gesture of choice.

12. Utilize that gesture and endeavor to conduct yourself in manner consistent with the transformed version of yourself. If you are unable to envision that scenario once more, conduct yourself in a similar manner as that individual and reestablish the anchor. Reiterate these instructions multiple times until you firmly establish your imagination and the desired gesture as interconnected. Whenever you engage in that particular gesture, you will experience an increased sense of concentration and self-assurance.

Engage in the consistent application of this technique on a daily basis in order to cultivate novel, constructive behaviors.

Another widely recognized and validated NLP strategy that can assist individuals in managing their emotional states for personal development is known as the 'Circle of Excellence.' Allow us to delve into this technique in our ensuing discussion.

Embarking On The Path Of Weight Loss

One of the most significant obstacles to embarking on a weight loss journey is the reluctance or unwillingness to confront the associated challenges. Weight reduction encompasses a sequential procedure comprising three distinct components. These encompass strategies such as reducing food intake, engaging in physical activity, and shifting one's cognitive approach. Your success will be determined by the former.

Refusal or Ideologies that hinder personal growth:
Commencing this expedition proves to be the most arduous stage, as perceived by a multitude. It is possible that you may be reluctant to acknowledge the imperative of weight loss,

notwithstanding the detrimental impact it may have on your health and emotional well-being. Upon effectively resolving these matters, you may veritably embark on your journey. Frequently, individuals embark on their weight loss aspirations with a predisposed anticipation of failure. Here is a suggested approach to alleviate that issue:

- Get yourself Ready: The most important part of starting your journey is to develop the correct attitude before beginning. If you are committed to the notion of attaining a more slender physique, you must consider the broader perspective. There may be numerous rationales for desiring this outcome, but it is worth noting that a portion of them might inadvertently impede progress. For instance, should you engage in this solely with the purpose of appeasing others, your steadfastness shall not endure.

• Establish a Catalogue: Initiate the process by crafting a comprehensive catalogue of motivations for shedding weight, consciously distinguishing those that reside in the realm of pleasing others. Compose an alternate inventory wherein the aforementioned components are excluded. This allocation is meant for your exclusive benefit; otherwise, your aspiration may diminish over time. Additionally, considering immediate and short-term benefits or incentives that can serve as motivation for making prudent choices in the present moment, such as the desire to consume a nutritious breakfast in order to experience a sense of well-being throughout the day, may prove beneficial. Please do list all the reasons that motivate you to initiate this endeavor.

• Verify your choice of language: Which language have you employed in this enumeration? Have you employed terms like "must" or "need to" to articulate your aspiration for weight loss? These expressions indicate an inclination towards burdensome duties rather than a genuine inner motivation, leading to an inherent tendency to resist them. If one is skeptical of this claim, one can evaluate its validity by assuming a seated position in close proximity to an alluring comestible, such as cheese fries or ice cream, and engaging in a mental exercise whereby the individual repeatedly affirms their inability to partake in the consumption of said food item. You will observe an intensification of your cravings. Review your list again and observe any occurrences where language of this nature has been employed. Next, replace the phrases containing "must" with positive reinforcement or expressions of desire.

Opting to Dedicate Oneself to Weight Reduction

If you are determined to overcome the initial emotional obstacles that you are likely to encounter,

Find solace in the notion that the commencement of any venture presents the greatest challenge. This phenomenon can be elucidated by scientific principles. The human brain is inherently programmed to carry out activities that have been ingrained into one's customary practices and routines.

- Familiarity breeds comfort: Within our minds lie cognitive shortcuts that facilitate our navigation through daily tasks, allowing us to preserve our mental resources. If we were to lack these cognitive heuristics, we would inevitably confront a state of inundation whereby even the most trivial choices would become burdensome throughout our daily routines. Nevertheless, there is a drawback associated with this scenario if we find ourselves entrenched in detrimental habits. Regrettably, a significant portion of individuals succumb to this innate tendency and discover that it operates to their detriment, rather than their benefit.

These cognitive heuristics can be understood as fundamental principles guiding the functioning of your mind, instructing you to trust and act upon instantaneous thoughts or ideas that arise spontaneously. To put it differently, established customs are preferable to alteration. One can perceive how this could be counterproductive in the pursuit of enhancing one's dietary habits. We gravitate towards the familiar, whether it be indulging in an additional slice of pie or reaching for a bag of chips, as it aligns with our customary actions, thus evoking a sense of correctness.

• Establishing Forward Motion: The sole approach to cease this pattern is to initiate a different trajectory that aligns more effectively with your goals, ultimately transforming it into a realm that you are accustomed to. Therefore, establishing a sense of momentum within our habits is the most effective approach to sustaining their continuity. An individual who leads a sedentary lifestyle is likely to remain idle, while an individual who is consistently active is likely to continue being active. Put differently, after adhering to your newly devised strategy for an extended duration, you will gradually develop a predilection for the modified behaviors and thought patterns. Upon grasping the inherent predisposition of the human mind towards familiarity, even when it may lead to unfavorable outcomes, one embarks on the path towards overcoming this impulse.

- Commence with modest steps: A more manageable approach entails addressing one stage at a time, instead of undertaking the entire endeavor from the outset. If your objective is to, for instance, enhance your physical fitness, initiate by engaging in a daily regimen of 10-minute walks. In due course, you will observe a desire to engage in lengthier periods of walking. Engaging in small positive actions is a way to align your efforts with your cognitive faculties, rather than opposing or hindering them.

Weekly Journal:
Prior to implementing any of the NLP techniques delineated in this book, it is imperative to engage in an initial exercise involving comprehensive documentation of all consumables and beverages consumed over a span of one week, alongside meticulous noting of the corresponding time of intake. Crucial: Refrain from employing any measures to impede or modify your regular eating habits throughout this designated week. Merely maintain your customary dietary routines, albeit with the additional caution of observing and documenting your actions.

- Practice Honesty and Provide Elaboration: Maintain your regular eating habits while devoting the necessary effort to document them thoroughly. If inadvertently omitting the recording of a meal occurs, it is permissible. Kindly jot it down at your earliest convenience. The greater level of specificity one can document, the higher degree of advantageous positioning one will gain in subsequent stages. Please ensure to make a record of all the beverages you consume.

- Enhanced awareness: This compilation of information holds immense value, as it will not only facilitate a heightened state of awareness regarding your consumption patterns, but also provide valuable insights into your specific habits. Often, individuals traverse through life making choices on autopilot, oblivious to the actions they are undertaking. The collective impact of those choices over an extended period molds and shapes our character. Gaining consciousness is the initial stage in embarking on your path of weight reduction.

After completing a week of recording, you may proceed to the following stages.

Strategic Method For Enhancing Self-Assurance

I am confident that you have completed the preceding exercise and transcribed the requested information. With that in mind, let us proceed to another exercise. Please take a moment to reflect on a matter in which you possess unwavering assurance, and imagine yourself embodying that very confidence at this moment. If you were to emanate confidence, what choices would you make regarding your stance or movement? Just pretend. What would be the quality or tone of your voice? How would you perceive yourself and what mental imagery do you associate with it?

Kindly repeat the action once more. Once more, envision yourself exuding confidence in your present state.

Consider your posture, movements, vocal tone, internal thoughts, and the mental imagery that arises. Just notice that. Recall the previous exercise in which I requested you to engage in negative thinking; the images presented were dissimilar.

When contemplating the notion of enhancing one's self-assurance, this sentiment arises within one's cognitive faculties. As a mere exercise, employing the power of imagination, let us entertain the notion of confidence and thus pretend to embody it. Engage in this exercise for a few additional repetitions, and subsequently, when you experience the gratifying sensation of self-assurance, observe the specific areas in which this sense of confidence is required. Envision yourself in a prospective scenario where you exude confidence and exhibit impeccable performance. Please complete this task promptly and subsequently proceed to the challenging exercises, which offer a much more impactful training experience in the upcoming sessions. Please execute this task, following which we shall progress to the subsequent instructional segment.

WHAT IS NLP ANCHORING?

NLP anchoring is widely regarded as one of the most prominent NLP techniques due to its tremendous efficacy and prompt effects. Through the utilization of NLP techniques, individuals possess the capacity to intentionally immerse themselves in a myriad of desired emotional states, such as happiness, confidence, serenity, and many more. easily.

Presented below is an illustrative example aimed at enhancing comprehension regarding the concept of NLP anchoring. The song serves as an anchor when we engage in it or partake in specific activities in a state of joy. This implies that each time we engage in the activity of listening to the same song or engaging in the same action as before, our level of happiness is restored. What is your perspective on the causation of this phenomenon? This occurrence is due to the inadvertent transformation of the song into an anchoring mechanism or activating stimulus. Now, whenever we happen to hear the same song, it elicits that same sensation of joy once more. Therefore, numerous positive and negative influences are generated throughout our lifetime. NLP enables us to utilize the positive occurrence as a foundation for establishing an anchor in subsequent situations.

Allow us to establish a foundation for joy. Herein, I present the sequential processes:

1. Recollect a Joyful Occasion from Your Previous Experiences: In order to establish a firm foundation of happiness, it is essential to first attain a state of contentment. Please recount a noteworthy occurrence or series of moments (from your personal history) that brought forth feelings of joy. Retrieve and gather all the pleasant

thoughts and images. Envision yourself and your cherished companions radiating joy, merriment, and similar expressions of delight.

2. Establish an Anchoring Technique: Upon successfully accessing and reliving pleasant memories from your personal history, and experiencing a resurgence of corresponding joy and contentment, it can be inferred that you have reached the pinnacle of your emotional state. At this juncture, deploy a distinct anchor; for instance, apply pressure to your left palm by pinching it. Please discharge the anchor a few more times (which involves squeezing your palm) while you are still experiencing the pinnacle of your emotional state.

Restore Your Composure and Return: It is essential for you to return and restore your composure by rising, engaging in physical movement, and dispelling your current state. Reiterate the process of anchoring once more. After engaging in several further repetitions of the exercise, the desired mental state will become firmly rooted and persistently accessible to you during times of necessity.

The Efficacy Of Communication Lies In The Reaction It Elicits.

The meaning:

Have you ever engaged in a communicative exchange where you endeavored to articulate and underscore a particular point to an individual, only to have them misunderstand or misconstrue your intended message? I frequently encounter such situations. I must admit that I initially attributed blame to them, erroneously presuming it to be their wrongdoing. However, upon careful reflection, I have come to realize that the responsibility for the matter lies squarely on my own shoulders.

Attempting to communicate with an individual encompasses more than mere verbal expression; it denotes the skill of effectively conveying one's intended meaning to the recipient.

An additional possibility entails encountering the situation in which an individual engages in dialogue with you. When there is a misunderstanding with him, it can be attributed to his deficiency in communication skills; however, it is also important to assist him by assuming the role of a attentive listener.

The course of action that you ought to pursue:

Recognize that in the event of a misinterpretation of your words by someone, it indicates the need for refinement in your communication skills. When engaging in discourse, it is imperative to accentuate and articulate your thoughts clearly, minimizing unnecessary dialogue as a protracted delivery can potentially disengage the listener, resulting in diminished receptivity.

A recommendation I would suggest is to initially endeavor to empathize with the individual you are conversing with, by putting yourself in their position. Consistently question whether the individual in question possesses a profound intellect, exhibits astuteness, or if they merely demonstrate unfamiliarity or lack of knowledge.

Furthermore, it would be advantageous for you to adjust your speech pace to allow him to comfortably follow along. It is also advisable to refrain from employing intricate vocabulary, solely for the purpose of appearing impressive.

It is advisable to prioritize active listening over speaking, as this approach facilitates a deeper understanding of the individual. Furthermore, if the opportunity presents itself, it is recommended to inquire and seek information rather than solely providing one's own insights. By posing questions, one grants the interlocutor the opportunity to engage in further reflection and potentially arrive at their own solutions. Conversely, embracing a questioning approach enables a greater comprehension of the individual in question through the acquisition of informative responses.

Allow me to provide you with a set of guidelines to become an attentive listener. Initially, endeavor to maintain focus on his statements. Establish visual contact with him and endeavor to mentally conjure vivid imagery of the concepts he is articulating to you. And refrain from interjecting while he is speaking, unless you wish to seek clarification or pose a question regarding any misunderstandings.

"The advantages that you will receive:

A good communicator possesses excellent charisma and an engaging personality, thereby avoiding the tendency to be perceived as a monotonous individual who incessantly rambles on in conversation. Furthermore, individuals will be inclined to confide in you, as you embody a profound respect for others and their viewpoints. This will undoubtedly lead to your success as a coach or mentor.

You will also be entitled to these benefits if you possess exceptional listening skills. You will garner favor and earn esteem from individuals by demonstrating perceptive and comprehensive comprehension of their needs during interpersonal engagements.

How To Substitute Negative Experiences With Positive Counterparts

Recontextualization refers to a cognitive transformation wherein one alters the context surrounding their life's events and phenomena, enabling them to emancipate themselves from past negative experiences and transmute them into positive ones.

Context refers to the inherent significance of an event or phenomenon, as discerned by individuals through representative systems.

You have the capability to break free from the impact of previous failures.

Do you find it convenient to access resource states?

It is likely that you have observed that in the context of training, when one finds oneself in a tranquil and secure setting, either in solitude or in the presence of trusted individuals, the task at hand becomes considerably more effortless. Though initial attempts may prove challenging, ultimately, everyone finds a way to manage this.

However, individuals often encounter challenges when attempting to willingly engage with resourceful states in their everyday existence. Particularly in circumstances where one encounters negative emotions, such as feelings of annoyance, concern, offense, or anger.

During such occasions, you might observe that it becomes exceedingly arduous to compel oneself to concentrate on affirmative imagery and immersing into a state of revitalization. This phenomenon is entirely inherent to nature. If your consciousness and subconscious mind are accustomed to non-resource states, then out of habit you will be drawn into it every time the situation resembles something from the past, when you have gained negative experience and experienced negative emotions.

The accumulation of past experiences leaves an indelible mark on our minds. Consequently, is humanity inevitably fated to perpetually relive past failures? Of course not. We can change that.

In order to accomplish this, one must possess the awareness that it is not any past experience that shapes us, but rather only certain events from our personal history, to which we attribute significant significance.

Frequently, individuals in previous times experienced both achievements and setbacks of equal proportion. However, he gave little regard to fortune. It appeared evident to him that this is self-evident. Possibly, he experienced delight upon obtaining his desired outcome, yet this sense of joy was rapidly overshadowed.

However, each instance of failure, no matter how trivial, carried the weight of a significant calamity for him. These setbacks lingered in his memory, leaving an indelible mark and leading him to draw profound conclusions about his own inadequacy. Despite achieving notable successes, including significant ones, they inexplicably failed to acknowledge his status as a successful individual.

As one may surmise, the crux of the matter pertains once more to the myriad distortions impeding our objective perception of the world's panorama. We possess a highly subjective perception, influenced by the lenses of our consciousness and subconscious, capturing not merely a comprehensive portrayal of the universe, but also the significance embedded within specific occurrences and phenomena. A similar phenomenon occurs in relation to our own personal experiences. We observe our own personality, behavior, and past through the lens of our consciousness, which inevitably leads to distortion.

Consequently, our perception extends beyond encompassing the entirety of reality, instead, it is limited to a specific fraction of it. As an illustration, one could observe a scenario wherein an individual solely embraces a reality in which they are deemed unsuccessful, subject to ridicule by all, or where their aspirations can solely be realized through arduous exertion, sacrifice, and forfeiture. Indeed, the scope of reality is considerably broader and characterized by significant variation. Each individual possesses immense capacities that far surpass our own perceptions. Many individuals frequently fail to recognize splendid prospects due to their self-imposed limitations imposed by their perceptual framework. Due to this particular framework, individuals may solely perceive challenges and obstacles, rather than recognizing the opportunities that can lead to their fortune. And for the very same rationale - due to the excessive emphasis he previously placed on challenges and the lack of attentiveness towards fortuitous opportunities, notably apparent ones, as well as his own competencies and advantageous attributes, that can lead to accomplishing success.

Indeed, previous occurrences are immutable and irrevocable. However, we have the ability to alter their perspective. It is a commonly held understanding that our perception constructs our perception of the world.

By altering our perception, we effectively transform our understanding of the world.

The Insights

Insight means understanding. Comprehending the true nature of the situation. In both individual cognition and collective perceptions. The purpose of NLP insights is to facilitate cognitive readiness for the matters to be addressed. These points encapsulate the essential elements of this preparation.

1) Prior to engaging in a particular circumstance, it is imperative to attain a suitable psychological and emotional disposition. The process is twofold. Primarily, it discusses strategies for readiness in foreseeable circumstances, and secondly, it explores approaches for preparedness and response in unforeseen circumstances, often the origin of anxiety and errors.

2) The most valuable resource available to assist you in monitoring your mind is the repository of memories that you possess. You are required to ascertain the memories that are relevant to each particular situation and extract the pertinent elements to utilize. The key lies in accessing the reservoir of your recollections and extracting the pertinent ones.

3) How frequently have you become frustrated with individuals who exhibit a confrontational demeanor? There exists a straightforward methodology whereby one can transform their reaction towards such individuals, shifting from an aggressive stance to one that is assertive.

4) Your cognition has established innate filters that operate autonomously to react to various moods and behaviors. It is required that you ascertain the

presence of these filters and make necessary adjustments to ensure their functionality serves a constructive purpose should they possess negative attributes.

5) In numerous instances, it may be necessary to assume an alternate persona and analyze a situation perspectively as an observer.

The underlying idea of the insights revolves around subjectivity. Each individual's perception is subjective, resulting in the creation of reproductions of this experience based on their unique set of values and beliefs. This recurrence is integral to characterizing the conduct. Hence, altering the perception from subjective to objective will result in a shift in behavioral tendencies.

NLP Methodology: Effective Message Delivery

One's actions or words are not the sole determining factor, but rather the manner in which they are carried out or expressed. Frequently, individuals do not perceive, hear, or comprehend the true intent or substance of a communication. The manner in which you conveyed the message typically evokes the response. The manner in which you express yourself carries equal significance to the content of your communication. It pertains to the distinction between communicating at and communicating with.

Acknowledge that you possess the capability and adaptability to adjust your communication approach. Adapt your methodology to align with the specific circumstances, the content, and the intended recipient of the communication. Additionally, make sure to make your modifications based on the individual's response. This necessitates the need for you to attentively observe not only their verbal answers but also their non-verbal indicators. This inherent flexibility greatly enhances your communication skills. It would bring great pleasure to individuals to engage in communication with you.

The difference in communicating

Initially, it is imperative to direct one's attention towards acquiring proficiency in NLP techniques, such as those aforementioned, with the objective of establishing a connection while engaging in communication. The focus should not lie on presenting oneself before an audience and showcasing one's capacity to effortlessly "discern thoughts" or subtly sway others. It does not solely entail illusion or sorcery, but rather encompasses a way of life aimed at enhancing communication and bolstering your self-assurance.

Authentic communication entails the vibrant interchange of ideas. The aim is to foster an engagement, rather than seeking applause or impressing others. After the commencement of communication, the primary emphasis lies in observing and analyzing the manner in which the other individual reciprocates throughout the entirety of the conversation. Furthermore, it is imperative to consider that the utmost priority lies in utilizing these outcomes or reactions as a means to modify one's communication style and message, in order to effectively convey the intended information to the individual.

The effectiveness of communication

The efficacy of communication hinges upon the aptitude to promptly receive and reciprocate the feedback provided by the interlocutor. This aligns with the principle of Natural Language Processing, where the significance of communication lies in the elicited response. Accompanying this NLP capsule is the cautionary note that the intended communication may not always align with the perception of the recipient.

Communicate with more awareness. Remain fully present and actively engage. I urge you to refrain from engaging in mindless chatter without considering the emotions and thoughts of the other individual. It will be evident to individuals if you demonstrate concern for their opinions and emotions. They would discern the underlying intent behind your meticulously crafted discourse. Strive to enhance your level of engagement, carefully considering and adapting to the evolving responses and changes that occur.

Refrain from manifesting any of the following personalities:

Individuals who disregard or neglect to acknowledge feedback, such as certain salespersons, customer service representatives, and inadequate managers, amongst others. Consider the instance when you encountered a sales representative who delivered their sales pitch insensitively, without taking into account the reactions and responses of prospective customers. People quickly lose interest. Have you made an attempt to actively engage in listening but have found yourself gradually losing focus? The aforementioned outcome will also ensue should you neglect to be vigilant in monitoring and adequately addressing feedback. Your audience will be swiftly lost. Indeed, while your delivery of the meticulously constructed message was impeccable, it regrettably fell short of eliciting the intended response or achieving the desired outcome. To what extent did the inability of numerous teams to attain their objectives result from their manager's provision of motivational speeches, frequent convening of meetings, and disregard for the input and feedback of team members?

Trainers who effectively delivered presentations and facilitated workshops demonstrated strong presentation skills, yet earned low evaluations. Although their presentation was outstanding and their workshop was meticulously organized, it regrettably did not align with the preferences or requirements of the customers. Despite being perhaps the most exceptional message available, the customers, regrettably, were unable to comprehend and effectively utilize it due to its presentation in unsuitable formats.

Aim for feedback-led communication. All parties involved will derive greater satisfaction and remarkably advance towards a mutually beneficial outcome by employing this highly effective methodology. "This methodology comprises of the subsequent course of actions:

Observe visible cues denoting alterations in demeanor or condition.

Perceive and acknowledge subtle vocal cues that signify a shift in one's condition or demeanor.

Kindly direct your attention towards the timely arrival of responses.

It is advisable to promptly respond as any delay may result in a missed opportunity, with the recipient's focus moving irreversibly elsewhere.

Convey the message in segmented increments or bite-sized portions, ensuring that the audience or recipient is not overwhelmed.

Utilizing The Technique Of Self-Hypnosis For Efficient Internal Communication

Self-hypnosis is a form of self-induced trance characterized by a state of altered consciousness, wherein one is not fully unconscious but rather in a sleep-like state, facilitating effortless communication with the subconscious mind in order to effect positive changes. By engaging in self-hypnosis, one can delve into their subconscious, comprehend their fears and beliefs, and subsequently modify them in a positive manner, thereby establishing an enhanced framework for personal growth. Allow me to elucidate the methodology for accomplishing this objective.

Methods for Implementing Self-Hypnosis Techniques

Commence with the donning of attire that is suited to ensure comfort, thus avoiding the continual adjustment of one's garments.

Seek solace in a serene and undisturbed environment, while reclining upon a couch or chair in a posture that brings you utmost comfort.

Consider your objectives for hypnosis; what is the reason behind your desire to induce self-hypnosis? Are you engaging in this activity with the sole intention of unwinding, or is there a specific objective in mind, such as imparting a particular message or enhancing proficiency in a specific domain? Reflect upon this matter to attain a deeper understanding of your objective in the realm of hypnosis, and proceed with deliberate efficacy in its pursuit.

After finalizing your hypnosis objectives, proceed to formulate a constructive affirmation focusing specifically on them. For example, should you desire to discontinue an unhealthy habit like smoking, your proposed statement could be, 'I opt to cease smoking as cigarettes no longer hold any allure for me.' Alternatively, if your aim is to cultivate a more optimistic mindset and reprogram your thoughts to focus on positivity, you may state, 'I embody a positive nature and consistently engage in constructive thinking, enabling me to lead a fulfilling life.' These suggestions are to be deliberately reiterated in order to firmly establish them in your subconscious. It is crucial to determine what thoughts you wish to instill in your mind, thereby directing its focus accordingly. Please ensure that the suggestion remains concise, optimistic, and unambiguous. The content should exclusively consist of positive words, as the human mind has a tendency to filter out language with negative connotations and adjust its interpretation accordingly. Consequently, when you express, 'I will not smoke', it is probable that your mind will disregard the 'not', resulting in the alteration of the suggestion to 'I will smoke'. Thus, it is advised to employ solely affirmative language in your suggestions. Additionally, maintain a focus on the present rather than fixating on the future, in order to foster a sense of accomplishment or progress towards your goal. To cultivate a sense of happiness in your life, it is advisable to employ the phrase 'I am happy' instead of 'I am going to be happy'. By doing so, you condition your mind to focus on the present state of happiness, thereby enabling yourself to experience positive emotions starting from today.

Subsequently, kindly shut your eyes and engage in a series of deep inhalations and exhalations in order to induce a state of mental relaxation. In the event that distressing thoughts arise, endeavor to take a more profound inhalation and subsequently release the negative thought as you engage in exhalation.

Recall a pleasant recollection or fix your attention on a specific spot on the wall, continuing to concentrate until a slight feeling of drowsiness ensues.

Recite 'I am experiencing an increase in eyelid weight and a sensation of drowsiness' silently to yourself, allowing these words to induce a genuine feeling of heaviness. By consistently voicing a suggestion, you reinforce its validity to your subconscious mind, thereby acknowledging its truth. In this manner, you prompt your subconscious to readily embrace the suggestion and induce a similar mode of operation. By consistently affirming statements such as 'I am happy' or 'I am feeling drowsy' to oneself, one gradually begins to perceive and undergo the corresponding effects. Recite the phrase "My eyelids are experiencing an increase in weight" repeatedly, and within a short span of time, you will perceive a sense of drowsiness and transition into a state resembling a trance.

Proceed to acknowledge any bodily tension, commencing from your toes and gradually ascending to the top of your head. Envision each and every component of your physique gradually alleviating weight and tension, as you exhale. Draw tranquility into your being as you breathe in, and release anxiety and strain with each exhalation you make.

You will experience a significant sense of relaxation at this juncture. To ensure optimal readiness for mental assimilation of your selected proposition, assess your state of hypnotic induction. Visualize the scenario in which you possess a halved lemon and proceed to exert pressure, extracting its juices directly into your oral cavity. Are you able to perceive the tangy flavor of it? What is your immediate response? Should you experience any perceptible bitter sensation in your oral cavity, it indicates that you have entered a state of deep concentration where your thoughts, perceptions, tastes, and imaginations are shaped by your own self-directed narrative.

Now, endeavor to attain a higher level of relaxation. Conceive of yourself ascending a staircase comprising of 10 steps until you reach the summit.

Envision the scenario wherein one descends the staircase, witnessing its immersion into water commencing from the fifth step onward. Continuously descend while mentally tallying the stride and concurrently envision a gradual immersion into water, wherein a deep sense of relaxation and tranquility ensues. At this juncture, you will begin to experience a heightened sense of relaxation.

It is highly probable that you will experience a mild sensation of numbness at this juncture, and if such sensation is not present, it is recommended to repeat the preceding two actions several additional times, until a state of numbness and relaxation is achieved.

Please regularly recite your selected suggestion in order to reinforce its impact in your mind. You have the option to vocalize it audibly or maintain internal repetition, preferably for a duration of 10 minutes. Prior to commencing your hypnosis session, it is recommended to establish a timer for a duration of 20 minutes.

Once you have recited the chosen affirmation (suggestion) for a substantial duration and feel prepared to conclude the hypnotic state, envisage yourself ascending the staircase while the water gradually recedes. Please proceed at your own pace while ascending the staircase and ensure that you maintain deep and steady breathing throughout the process.

Upon reaching the concluding phase, gradually open your eyes and envision transitioning from the hypnotic state to the tangible realm. Alternatively, one may express this sentiment in a more formal tone by stating, "One may also employ phrases such as 'I am fully alert' or 'I have regained consciousness' intermittently to readily reorient oneself to actuality."

Now ponder upon your sentiments regarding the self-improvement you aspire to achieve, and you shall experience a remarkable enthusiasm in relation to it.

Engage in the daily application of this particular method in order to effectively convey the intended messages to your mind, thereby prompting it to adopt predetermined patterns of cognition and behavior. This enables you to cultivate self-assurance, tranquility, serenity, composure, optimism, drive, and concentration, thereby enabling you to attain all your objectives.

Now, let us proceed to the subsequent chapter and explore further strategies for influencing the mind with you.

How To Deal With Fear

One might believe that there is a multitude of strategies that can be employed to enhance one's professional trajectory, provided they assert themselves more effectively. If you are experiencing difficulty in terms of cultivating confidence, rest assured. You are not the sole individual grappling with issues pertaining to self-worth.

The Challenge of Social Anxiety

Are you aware that public speaking is regarded as the foremost fear among individuals in the United States? This implies that individuals experience a greater degree of apprehension when it comes to public speaking compared to their fear of mortality. Statistics indicate that approximately 75% of the populace experiences a significant level of trepidation when faced with the need to engage in interpersonal communication. The phenomenon known as glossophobia, which denotes an intense apprehension towards engaging in public speaking, is classified as a subtype of social anxiety.

Social anxiety is widely recognized as the apprehension associated with being required to interact with individuals, particularly in collective settings. This occurs when an individual experiences a sense of apprehension or unease towards the individuals with whom they are required to interact with. This apprehension is primarily encountered by individuals who have undergone the incidence of being subjected to humiliation or rejection perpetrated by others. The prevalence of making errors in public or facing rejection is a universal experience, substantiating the probability that individuals known to you might demonstrate shyness or a strong aversion towards public presentations.

What Causes This Fear?

Although there may have been occurrences of rejections and mistakes in the past, the human brain possesses the ability to recall a painful memory whenever confronted with a comparable occurrence. Take, for instance, the situation where one has encountered extreme embarrassment during a formal conference. It is highly probable that this individual will subsequently link any future instances of attending conferences to that very distressing occurrence. Regardless of whether you have acquired the necessary skills to avoid repeating the same error, your mind will still present you with a vivid mental image of being in an undesirable situation. Consequently, you experience profound unease whenever confronted with the prospect of participating in a meeting that encompasses the chief executive officers of all the companies with which you would be affiliating.

Upon careful examination of this specific fear, one can readily observe its lack of logical coherence. Nevertheless, due to your failure to challenge the cognitive linkages formed by your mind, you persist in residing within this state of apprehension. It is possible that you possess the comprehension that errors are part of the human experience and can serve as opportunities for growth and learning. However, due to the cognitive associations that have formed in your mind, you find it difficult to demonstrate self-compassion. When an individual's mental faculties impede the ability to engage in constructive self-affirmation due to persistent memories of previous instances of rejection, a sense of resentment and powerlessness ensues, despite possessing the capability to address the situation independently.

What You Can Do

Given your understanding of the issue lying within the connection forged by your mind, it becomes evident that the appropriate course of action would involve altering your perspective of said association. "Allow me to provide you with the following instructions:

Consider the daunting circumstances that might underlie your social anxiety or apprehension. This could be an instance in which you were subjected to ridicule and humiliation previously, or an occasion in which you experienced a sense of embarrassment and self-deprecation. Carefully analyze all the intricate aspects that your cognition captures, along with the emotional response evoked from envisioning that specific scenario.

Now, envision yourself observing that scene within the confines of a cinematic venue. Carefully envision the scene, yet in addition, observe the intricate aspects of the theater, such as the curtains positioned next to the screen, the seat upon which you envisage yourself seated, and the texture of the flooring beneath your feet. You will perceive a pronounced sense of spatial detachment in the mental realm you inhabit, yet the vibrancy of the imaginary setting is impeccably preserved, owing to the intricate array of visual and auditory particulars that envelop you within this fictitious theatrical domain.

Envision a scenario wherein the audio of the film you are presently viewing is no longer audible. Furthermore, desaturate the scenes. Presently, the mental picture you are envisioning bears a striking resemblance to a monochromatic, silent motion picture, reminiscent of a production from the 1940s. You may experience a sense of disconnection from the film, perhaps even recognizing a diminished level of interest in it.

Envision a pleasant scenario, such as the possibility of receiving a salary increase following your upcoming performance evaluation, or even more desirable, a promotion. Envision the scenario with your presence, as though you are personally immersed in it. Encourage your mind to generate an abundance of intricate details.

Whenever you find yourself experiencing bouts of anxiety, it is recommended to repeatedly engage in this NLP exercise. In a brief period, you will grasp the ability to dismiss any detrimental thoughts concerning your fears effortlessly.

NLP Within Business

Similarly, when discussing the aforementioned, numerous individuals struggle with the demands of sales acquisition. In order to effectively engage in sales, it is imperative to ascertain the genuine level of interest that prospective customers possess towards the product prior to making any attempts at persuasion or promotion. By leveraging the capabilities of Natural Language Processing, however, you can commence to gain a competitive advantage.

If you tend to become unresponsive when asked questions or encounter difficulty in formulating sales messages that resonate with clients and drive purchase decisions, you should contemplate employing NLP techniques to overcome these challenges. By doing so, you can pave the way for future advancement and make meaningful strides towards progress.

Could you kindly specify the requisite competencies necessary for excelling as a proficient entrepreneur who operates in synergy with inherent qualities and talents?

• Self-assurance

• Magnetic presence or charm

• Familiarity with the product • Understanding of the product • Proficiency in product information • Comprehensive knowledge of the product

• A lucid explication • Exemplary articulation • Impeccable elucidation • Precision in elucidation • Profound clarity • Meticulous explanation • Eloquent exposition

• The capacity to transmit knowledge

Undoubtedly, an adept salesperson possesses the ability to effectively engage with even the most curt and confrontational clientele, swiftly transforming their demeanor into one of amusement and lighthearted banter.

Less charismatic or natural sales members will look on enviously as the silver-tongued expert gets even the most challenging of sales put through.

In due course, they acquire the individual's accounts of their children and personal life, establishing a level of familiarity as though their bond had endured for a considerable period of time.

If you possess the capability to utilize NLP, however, you can gradually work towards affording this type of personality an opportunity to manifest within yourself. What measures can one take to ensure that individuals enjoy one's humor? Follow your presentations? Initiate appropriate measures upon inquiry.

• To enhance one's performance in the realm of sales, it is beneficial to promptly recognize the value of Neuro-linguistic Programming (NLP) in enabling sales professionals to craft humorous remarks that elicit laughter, and to develop the self-assurance necessary to pose incisive inquiries that yield the requisite answers for closing a deal. NLP will prioritize understanding the clients' motivations as a fundamental step prior to undertaking any efforts to promote the product to them.

Additionally, NLP proves to be highly effective for professionals in the realm of human resources. It aids in effectively identifying the most suitable candidate for the position, as well as navigating challenging questions in order to ultimately secure the most proficient personnel. Other Human Resources professionals may not feel as at ease with probing an interviewee; Natural Language Processing (NLP) will aid them in reaching a stage in which they will consistently ask the most incisive and demanding inquiries.

- Finally, executives in the business realm can greatly benefit from leveraging NLP techniques as it enhances their comprehension of individuals. Therefore, the process of selling is facilitated through the implementation of effective presentation tactics, adept communication with other stakeholders, and, critically, efficient organization and preparation of the business to align with its intended operations.

• Business-oriented courses focusing on NLP are readily available, thus necessitating vigilance in identifying such opportunities. Similarly, it is imperative to acknowledge that significant time investment is required. If you aspire to refine yourself or a member of your business into an ideal candidate for the job, it should be noted that NLP requires a significant investment of time to achieve desired outcomes and yield tangible results.

Please be prepared for an extended waiting period, as the outcomes have the potential to bring about significant changes and facilitate sustained, enduring accomplishments.

www.ingramcontent.com/pod-product-compliance
Lightning Source LLC
Chambersburg PA
CBHW050238120526
44590CB00016B/2134